W9-AZC-855

PORT

Pue

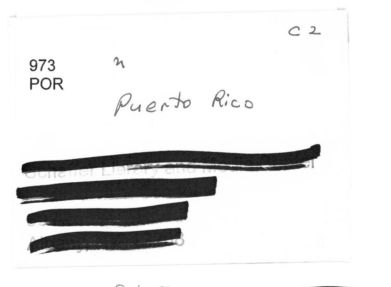

Steck-Vaughn Company

Executive Editor	Diane Sharpe
Senior Editor	Martin S. Saiewitz
Design Manager	Pamela Heaney
Photo Editor	Margie Foster

Proof Positive/Farrowlyne Associates, Inc.
Program Editorial, Revision Development, Design, and Production

Reviewer: Rafael A. Filardi, Director of Economic Research

Published by Raintree Steck-Vaughn Publishers, an imprint of Steck-Vaughn Company.

A Turner Educational Services, Inc. book. Based on the Portrait of America television series by R. E. (Ted) Turner.

Cover Photo: San Juan by © Superstock.

Library of Congress Cataloging-in-Publication Data

Thompson, Kathleen.
    Puerto Rico / Kathleen Thompson.
      p.   cm. — (Portrait of America)
    "Based on the Portrait of America television series" — T.p.   verso.
    "A Turner book."
    Includes index.
    ISBN 0-8114-7384-8 (library binding).
    ISBN 0-8114-7465-8 (softcover).
      1. Puerto Rico—Juvenile literature. I. Portrait of America (Television program) II. Title.
III. Series: Thompson, Kathleen. Portrait of America.
F1958.3.T46 1996
972.95—dc20
                                       95-38247
                                        CIP
                                        AC

Printed and Bound in the United States of America

3 4 5 6 7 8 9 10 WZ 04 03 02 01 00

Acknowledgments
The publishers wish to thank the following for permission to reproduce photographs:
P. 7 © Suzanne Murphy-Larronde/DDB Stock Photography; pp. 8, 10 © P. Dale Ware/DDB Stock Photography; p. 11 (left) © J. Messerschmidt/Tony Stone Images, (right) Puerto Rico Tourism Company; pp. 12, 14 (left) Columbus Memorial Library; p. 14 (bottom) Puerto Rico Tourism Company; p. 15 © Suzanne Murphy-Larronde/DDB Stock Photography; p. 16 UPI/Bettmann; p. 17 San Juan Star; pp. 18, 19 Puerto Rico Tourism Company; pp. 20, 21 © Miami Herald/Angel Valentin; p. 22 © Robert Frerck/Odyssey Productions; p. 23 © Suzanne Murphy-Larronde/DDB Stock Photography; p. 24 Gary A. Comer/DDB Stock Photography; p. 26 Medtronics, Inc.; p. 27 (top) Department of Agriculture, Commonwealth of Puerto Rico, (bottom) Puerto Rico Tourism Company; p. 28 Pfizer Inc.; p. 29 (top) Medtronics, Inc.; p. 29 (bottom), p. 30 Puerto Rico Tourism Company; p. 31 Arecibo Observatory/Cornell University/National Science Foundation; p. 32 © Suzanne Murphy-Larronde/DDB Stock Photography; p. 34 UPI/Bettmann; pp. 35, 36, 37 Puerto Rico Tourism Company; pp. 39, 40 © Suzanne Murphy-Larronde/DDB Stock Photography; p. 41 Puerto Rico Tourism Company; p. 42 © Miami Herald; p. 44 © W. Lynn Seldon, Jr./DDB Stock Photography; p. 46 One Mile Up; p. 47 (both) © Photo Researchers.

STECK-VAUGHN

PORTRAIT OF AMERICA

Puerto Rico

Kathleen Thompson

A Turner Book

RSVP

RAINTREE
STECK-VAUGHN
PUBLISHERS

The Steck-Vaughn Company

Austin, Texas

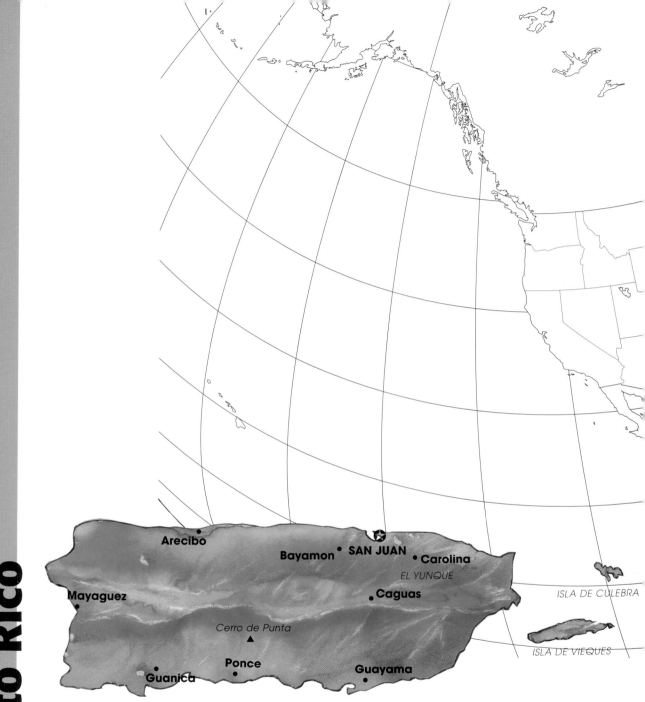

Puerto Rico

Arecibo

Bayamon • SAN JUAN
• Carolina
EL YUNQUE

Mayaguez

Caguas

Cerro de Punta
▲

Ponce

Guanica

Guayama

ISLA DE CULEBRA

ISLA DE VIEQUES

Contents

Introduction

From the air, Puerto Rico appears as a small, perfect rectangle floating on the Caribbean Sea. To the west lie larger islands. Tiny patches of land trail off to the east and south. A closer view shows emerald mountains, sparkling beaches, and tangles of modern roads—a variety of landscapes, natural and human, old and new. Here the world's largest radio telescope scans the sky only a few miles from a park where the island's first people worshiped eight hundred years ago. Here are high-rises finished only yesterday. Nearby stand some of the earliest buildings constructed by Europeans in the Western Hemisphere. A commonwealth of the United States, Puerto Rico brings to our nation gifts of technological know-how and a unique cultural heritage.

This house is in San Juan, the capital of Puerto Rico.

Puerto Rico

Columbus to Commonwealth

When Christopher Columbus landed at Puerto Rico in 1493, he encountered a Native American group called the Taino. These people were part of a larger group called the Arawak. The Arawak also inhabited parts of what are now Cuba and the Caribbean Islands. The Taino lived in houses built of logs and poles with thatched roofs. Some villages numbered three thousand people or more. Their main crops were cassava and corn (maize). They hunted birds and other small animals and fished. The Taino made jewelry, sometimes made of gold, that they wore in ceremonies. They also worked skillfully at pottery and basket making.

One of the men who served under Columbus, Ponce de León, came back to settle the island in 1508. The Spanish expected the Taino to pay tribute in gold and food in return for religious instruction. In 1511 the Taino rebelled, and many of them were killed. The rest were put to work mining for gold.

This statue honors Christopher Columbus. He visited Puerto Rico in 1493 on his second voyage from Spain.

This statue of Luis Muñoz Rivera is part of the Cathedral of Guadalupe in the central plaza in Ponce.

The Taino began dying in great numbers from disease and overwork. As they died, they were replaced with Native Americans from nearby islands and slaves from Africa.

In the 1530s the Spanish colonists began growing crops. Besides sugar cane, they grew a little cotton, ginger, cacao, and indigo. By the middle of the sixteenth century, the colony was having hard luck. It was constantly being raided by pirates and Native Americans from neighboring islands. Plagues wiped out much of the population, and colonists began deserting the island.

At that time England, France, and the Netherlands all had claimed some of the islands that surrounded Puerto Rico. It wasn't long before Spain realized that the little island of Puerto Rico was going to need protection. The Spanish tried to make the island impenetrable. Two huge fortresses were built on the ports at either side of the island. A stone wall 25 feet high and 18 feet thick ringed the coastline.

In 1595 Sir Francis Drake, the English explorer, attacked the island but was driven off. The English did capture the port of San Juan in 1598 but held it for only a few months before disease forced them to leave. The Dutch attacked in 1625 and were defeated, but only after San Juan had been burned. There were other

El Morro was one of the fortresses Spain built to protect Puerto Rico. It guarded the entrance to the harbor at San Juan.

Here, El Morro is pictured from the inside. After El Morro was built, Spain added to San Juan's defenses by building a 25-foot-high stone wall around the city.

These workers are harvesting sugar cane, one of Puerto Rico's leading crops.

attacks by the English in the early 1700s, but all were unsuccessful.

In 1765 a census reported that there were 45,000 people living on Puerto Rico. About five thousand of these people were slaves. Most of the land was in Spanish hands. Spanish settlers clustered around the walled port towns, especially San Juan. At about this time, the Spanish throne decided that all goods shipped from Puerto Rico should come to Spain. The farming communities of the interior of the island ignored the declarations of the Spanish Crown. They continued to trade goods with other countries.

By the end of the eighteenth century, there were many towns on the island. The population boomed to over 150,000 people. Immigrants brought new ideas and modern agricultural methods. Relations between Spain and Puerto Rico improved. Spain invested money and sent slaves into the colony. In 1804 the ports were officially opened to foreign ships for the first time.

Emperor Napoleon Bonaparte of France conquered Spain in 1808. Spanish colonies in Central and South America immediately asserted their right to independence. Puerto Rico, on the other hand, remained loyal to Spain's new government. In fact, many Spanish people from South and Central America who wished to remain loyal to Spain came to live in San Juan. These Spanish loyalists were given free land. Spain rewarded Puerto Rico's loyalty in 1815 by lifting trade restrictions. Now the island had permission to ship goods to non-Spanish countries, such as the United States.

Puerto Rico's small farm communities grew into plantations after 1830. Successful landowners bought and controlled smaller surrounding farms. Slaves were used to grow and harvest crops on the huge plantations. Landowners grew three primary crops: tobacco, coffee, and sugar cane. Most of the money gained from the sale of these products went to the Spanish government. The United States was Puerto Rico's main customer for sugar. However, coffee was the main source of income overall.

From 1837 to 1868, Puerto Ricans wanted to be represented in and governed by the Spanish legislature. In 1868 steps were taken toward changing Puerto Rico. A Puerto Rican commission voted to abolish slavery. The Spanish government was shocked and sensed that the islanders were preparing themselves for a rebellion. Puerto Rico was declared a province in

Luis Muñoz Rivera worked for greater Puerto Rican freedom around the turn of the century.

1868, giving it a little more voice in its own government. Slavery was abolished in 1873.

By the 1880s Román Baldorioty de Castro was leading a movement toward self-government, or autonomy. Riots broke out when the Spanish government sent soldiers in to stop the rebellion. This made the rebels want change even more, and the Autonomist party was eventually born. The leader of this party was Luis Muñoz Rivera. Working closely with the Liberal party in Spain in 1897, Rivera and the Autonomist party were able to gain a greater measure of self-government for Puerto Rico. The new government was never put into effect.

A few months later, a war broke out between the United States and Spain. Very little fighting occurred on Puerto Rico. Most of the battles took place on Cuba. However, the American Navy attacked the fortress at San Juan and came ashore at Guanica. The

San Juan is full of historic buildings. Many buildings in Old San Juan, like the ones pictured here, have been restored.

Spanish-American War ended in ten weeks. In the Treaty of Paris, Spain signed over Cuba, Guam, the Philippine Islands, and Puerto Rico to the United States. The island was a colony again.

After a short period of military government, the United States created a civil government. There was an elected legislature, but the governors were appointed by the President of the United States. The governor had complete power over the legislature. The governor's main objective was to make Puerto Rican finances, culture, and politics resemble America's.

The United States built highways, hospitals, dams, and schools. In 1917 the Jones Act made all Puerto Ricans citizens of the United States. Free trade was allowed between Puerto Rico and the United States. The big prize, as far as the United States was concerned, was the sugar market. Between 1899 and 1939, United States investors poured money into the sugar industry, while other crops, such as coffee and tobacco, were neglected. The owners of the sugar cane plantations became rich while the workers stayed poor.

Hacienda Buena Vista is a restored coffee plantation in Ponce, Puerto Rico. In the nineteenth century, coffee provided Puerto Rico with most of its income.

For years, the biggest political question in Puerto Rico had to do with what kind of government it should have. Some Puerto Ricans wanted complete independence. Some wanted statehood. Some wanted self-government but with strong ties to the United States.

In 1940 Luis Muñoz Marín, the son of Luis Muñoz Rivera, organized the Popular Democratic party. Muñoz Marín believed that the type of government Puerto Rico had was not as important as economic reform. It was time, he said, for Puerto Ricans to try to create a better standard of living for themselves. He wanted land reform, more industry, and more variety in the crops grown. Puerto Ricans deserved better health, education, and welfare.

In 1947 the United States Congress voted for an amendment that allowed Puerto Rico to elect its own governor. Muñoz Marín won the election in 1948 and served a total

Puerto Rico's constitution is modeled after the United States Constitution. This is Puerto Rico's capitol building in San Juan.

of four terms. The Popular Democratic party controlled the government of Puerto Rico for twenty years. During that time the Puerto Ricans changed their economy from one based on agriculture to one based on industry. Many workers left the fields and moved to the cities where better jobs and living conditions helped them improve their standard of living. Others migrated to the industrial cities in the United States, especially New York City.

In 1950 the United States Congress passed Public Law 600, which allowed Puerto Rico to write its own constitution. On July 25, 1952, the island became a commonwealth. The commonwealth status gave Puerto Rico the right to govern itself, while still being a part of the United States. The people maintained their American citizenry, but they still could not vote in United States elections. Taxes were paid to their own government, not to the United States. Free trade continued between the mainland and the island.

In 1962 Muñoz Marín, while serving his fourth term as governor, came to an agreement with President John F. Kennedy. A committee was set up to study the three possible types of government for Puerto Rico—statehood, independence, or an improved commonwealth. The committee reported that all three options were good ones and that the people should decide.

Luis Muñoz Marín was one of Puerto Rico's most creative statesmen.

At one time, the island of Puerto Rico was called San Juan, and the city that is now San Juan was called Puerto Rico. After hundreds of years, the names were reversed.

In 1967 a vote was taken in Puerto Rico. More than 65 percent of the registered voters participated. The result was 60.5 percent in favor of an improved commonwealth, 38.9 percent in favor of statehood, and 0.6 percent in favor of independence. President Lyndon Johnson declared that he was ready to form a committee to see how the commonwealth could be improved. The committee would include Puerto Ricans appointed by the governor.

By this time, however, Muñoz Marín was no longer governor. He had chosen not to run for a fifth term. Muñoz Marín's administrative assistant Roberto Sánchez Vilella was elected governor. He neglected to appoint Puerto Rico's half of the new committee. In 1968 Puerto Rico was controlled by a new party, the New Progressive party. The new governor, Luis Ferré, did send a committee to Washington, D.C. The committee asked for only one change. They wanted Puerto Ricans to vote in national elections. Congress did not accept their proposal.

Throughout the 1970s and the 1980s, support for statehood for Puerto Rico grew almost as strong as that for commonwealth. The pro-independence movement remained relatively small. The Popular Democratic party returned to power in 1972 but lost the following election to the pro-statehood party. The Popular Democratic party, under the leadership of Rafael Hernández Colón, then regained and held power for most of the 1980s.

In November 1993, almost five hundred years to the day after Columbus claimed the island for Spain, Puerto Ricans returned to the polls to express their desires about the status of their land. Although Governor Pedro Rosselló was eager for Puerto Rico to become the fifty-first state, the people voted to remain a commonwealth. This time, about 46 percent of the voters had supported statehood, with 4.4 percent voting for complete independence.

Since Columbus first landed on Puerto Rico, this island has become home for more than 3.5 million people of Spanish, Native American, and African heritage. The beautiful mountains and beaches remain, but today they exist side by side with shopping centers and fast-food restaurants. Many young Puerto Ricans rush off to the mainland to look for jobs. Tourists fly in to enjoy the sunshine. Life in Puerto Rico has become a fascinating mixture of new and old, of American and Spanish culture, of tradition and progress.

The port of San Juan developed rapidly after Spanish explorer Juan Ponce de León founded the original town of Caparra, in 1508. These buildings are in Old San Juan.

The Constant Question

The great majority of Puerto Ricans agree that they have a culture and way of life they want to preserve. They also want the island's economy to be strong and stable, with good jobs and economic security for their families. What status will best allow them to accomplish these goals? Should Puerto Rico be a state, a commonwealth, or an independent nation? This is the island's constant question.

The latest attempt to answer it came in 1993. In a nonbinding election, the people chose to remain a commonwealth. Those who support this status believe that it combines the best of both statehood and independence. Under the commonwealth, Puerto Ricans are United States citizens and can take part in national aid programs. Yet they don't have to pay federal taxes. They are free to maintain their language and their culture.

Commonwealth supporters were joined in opposing statehood by another group. Small but sometimes

Puerto Rico has four main political parties, making it more politically diverse than most of the United States. These voters support keeping Puerto Rico as a commonwealth.

loud, this group wants Puerto Rico to cut its ties with the United States. They want to go it alone as an independent nation. They argue that independence is the only status that will allow their people to remain Puerto Ricans.

But supporters of statehood believe that Puerto Rico would do best as a state. They think that Puerto Ricans deserve to be represented in the United States House and Senate and to vote in national elections. They do not think statehood would prevent Puerto Ricans from continuing to celebrate their own unique cultural traditions. They fear that if Puerto Rico is not a full-fledged state, the United States may someday take away the people's citizenship and special privileges. Supporters of statehood and those who favor the commonwealth agree about one thing. They both believe that full independence will mean greater poverty for their island. Without Puerto Rico's special ties to the United States, manufacturers might close down their factories there.

Historically, models for each status have existed throughout the world. For example, Texas and Hawaii were once

In San Juan, a commonwealth supporter waves a banner calling commonwealth status "the best of two worlds" — a compromise between independence and statehood.

independent republics. Australia and Canada have long held commonwealth status within the United Kingdom.

The constant question is a compli- cated one that only the people of Puerto Rico can answer. Anyone who watches trends is aware of a change. In 1967 statehood received about 39 percent of the vote. In 1993 this percentage climbed to 46.2 percent. The next time Puerto Ricans go to the polls, they may well vote to ask the United States Congress to make them the fifty-first state.

Home Is in the Highlands

For four hundred years, the *jíbaros* have lived in the mountains of Puerto Rico. The jíbaros are descendants of Native Americans and Spanish horsemen. Because they were alone up in the mountains, the jíbaros developed their own culture. They were able to support themselves by growing coffee beans, either for trade or to sell. The jíbaros' legendary strength and independence made them folk heroes to the rest of Puerto Rico.

Then the large sugar corporations came into Puerto Rico. Sugar was king, and coffee became less important. For the first time in their history, the

Farmers in Puerto Rico's Cordillera Central Mountains have been growing crops for hundreds of years.

This home is located high in the mountains of Puerto Rico.

people of the highlands could not make enough money to support their families. Many of the jíbaros went to work in the cane fields. Many others left for the mainland United States to find jobs. Sometimes families had to split up. Grandparents and young grandchildren traveled to cities like New York and Chicago, while parents and older children remained on the farm. Sometimes the jíbaros returned to Puerto Rico. One who came back expressed his desire to stay in his native land. "I love this place because I have more freedom," he said. "I can do my work, pick coffee, work with the chickens, cows, horses. Everything that has to do with nature, I love to do."

The mountain farmers do not have much land. Their income is not high. But it doesn't make sense to compare the cash they bring in with the wages of a factory worker or an office clerk. They have something else. The jíbaros live every day with the beauty of the highlands. They have the peacefulness of their land and its farms and mountains.

Up by the Bootstraps

For centuries Puerto Rico had been ruled by a foreign power. During most of the island's colonial period, both under Spain and the United States, Puerto Ricans had not had an opportunity to make life in Puerto Rico better.

In the 1940s the people of Puerto Rico began to "pull themselves up by their bootstraps." Operation Bootstrap was a creative self-help program led by Puerto Rican leader Luis Muñoz Marín. Operation Bootstrap succeeded in completely changing the economy of Puerto Rico.

The government of Puerto Rico, with the cooperation of the United States, instituted land reforms. Land that was held illegally by American sugar companies was given back to the people. But these land reforms were not successful in giving more people jobs.

The most effective part of Operation Bootstrap had to do with manufacturing. Puerto Rico Senate majority leader Roberto Rexach explained how the program worked. "The whole idea of Operation

Besides being Puerto Rico's capital, San Juan is the economic center of the island. This is part of the business district in downtown San Juan.

Bootstrap was to bring in what we didn't have—that's capital—so with that capital we could put to work what we really had—labor. At the time, it was inconceivable to industrialize a Caribbean island. So what did we do? Well, we set up three or four industrial operations. We brought in people from the states—investors. We showed them the island. We showed them our scenery, and then we showed them how well factories were run by Puerto Ricans. And then we invited them to come in, and they usually did."

The plan worked. Before Operation Bootstrap, Puerto Rico was very poor. It was nicknamed "The Poorhouse of the Caribbean." Today, all that has changed. Puerto Rico has one of the highest incomes per person of any area in Latin America.

Manufacturing, which turned the economy around, is still the largest part of the economy. There are about two thousand factories employing 166,000 workers. These workers produce more than forty percent of the total value of Puerto Rico's products and services. In the 1960s the island's Economic Development Administration—*Fomento* in Spanish—decided to push high-technology industries. As a result, Puerto Rico's most valuable products are chemicals—especially medicines—and electrical equipment, such as computers

This worker helps to produce pacemakers in a plant operated by Medtronic, Inc., one of Puerto Rico's technology companies.

Coffee is one of Puerto Rico's most important crops.

and pacemakers. Puerto Ricans also make food products, clothing, and scientific instruments.

Before 1955 agriculture was the most important part of the island's economy. It now accounts for only one percent of the total amount of goods and services produced on the island. About 33,000 people are employed in agriculture. They produce sugar cane and coffee, which are Puerto Rico's leading crops. Milk, poultry, and eggs are among the island's most valuable agricultural products. Tobacco and fruits of many kinds are also important commercial crops. Puerto Rico's climate makes it possible to grow tropical fruits, such as bananas, plantains, and pineapples, that can't thrive in other parts of the United States.

Pineapples are grown mainly in northern Puerto Rico's coastal lowlands. These men are selling pineapples from a roadside stand.

A technician inspects capsules of medication.

Farming is important in another way, too. There are a lot of small farms where farmers grow enough to feed their families and a little more. They don't show up much in the statistics on production and national income. But they are important to the culture. They prove that it is possible to make a living without working for someone else. And they keep alive a feeling for the land.

Service industries, which include everything from real estate to tourism, form the largest part of Puerto Rico's economy. For example, tourism alone brings in $1.5 billion a year. Visitors from the mainland can travel to this beautiful Caribbean island without passports. They can experience the rich culture of the island with all the comforts of home.

Through the years, growth in the island's economy has made a big change in the Puerto Rican way of life. Today, about ninety percent of the people can read and write. Children are required to go to school from the ages of 6 to 16. Three quarters of Puerto Rico's workers now have 12 years of education. Unemployment is still much higher in Puerto Rico than in the rest of the United States, so vocational schooling is being emphasized to reduce unemployment. Vocational schools train students in certain job skills.

Puerto Rico has taken more control of its own fate with Operation Bootstrap. Only time will tell how this feeling of independence may change the face of Puerto Rico.

above. High-tech industry is a leading part of Puerto Rico's economy.

below. Tourists are attracted to Puerto Rico for its tropical climate and beautiful beaches. In recent years, tourism has developed into one of Puerto Rico's major industries.

Where Planets Are Seen

Most of us have looked at the night sky and wondered about the stars. How is it that scientists know so much about space? How have they seen what most of us cannot?

Astronomy is the science that studies objects outside Earth's atmosphere. Where do astronomers go when they have questions about space? They may go to Arecibo, Puerto Rico.

The city of Arecibo is a large seaport in northern Puerto Rico. It was founded in 1616 near the mouth of the Arecibo River. It is a major trading port known for its manufacturing. However, astronomers think of it as home to the Arecibo Observatory. The world's largest single-unit radio telescope can be found there.

The Arecibo Observatory was built in the 1960s to help scientists conduct important space research. For example, scientists have produced detailed maps of the surface of Venus. They have also learned exactly how Venus rotates. The Arecibo telescope has helped astronomers learn about neutron stars.

The Arecibo telescope is often used to study pulsars and quasars. Pulsars are radio waves that are transmitted by collapsed stars. Quasars are a type of galaxy that sends a large amount of energy away from a small amount of space.

It has taught them about the movement of Earth.

How does the Arecibo Observatory radio telescope work? The atmosphere of Earth is transparent to light. That is why, for example, we can see the sun. In 1931 astronomers learned our atmosphere was also open to radio waves. Radio waves are much longer than light waves. So radio telescopes must be much larger than optical telescopes. Radio telescopes detect radiation emitted by planets, stars, galaxies, and quasars. Such telescopes give scientists another way to study space.

Radio telescopes, like the one at Arecibo, must have moveable dishes. Picture a satellite dish used for television reception like you might see in your neighbor's backyard. Now imagine that satallite dish HUGE! The dish at Arecibo is one thousand feet across. It can be steered in different directions. You might adjust your television to get a station more clearly. So moving the telescope ensures the best reception for astronomers. Using the antenna of the telescope, astronomers track Earth's movement. They also track the movement of other planets and stars.

The telescope at Arecibo has an ideal location. It lies level in a rounded-out hollow in the mountains. The telescope is made of perforated aluminum panels. These panels focus the radio waves toward the antenna. In this way astronomers can track the movement of objects in the sky.

The Arecibo observatory also has a smaller telescope. It is only one hundred feet across. It is used mostly to study the atmosphere of Earth. Between the two telescopes, Arecibo has a lot to offer astronomers. The next time you hear something interesting about space, think of Arecibo. It is entirely possible that the astronomers in Puerto Rico may be responsible for providing you with the latest fact.

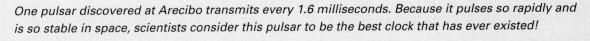

One pulsar discovered at Arecibo transmits every 1.6 milliseconds. Because it pulses so rapidly and is so stable in space, scientists consider this pulsar to be the best clock that has ever existed!

The Art of a Nation

In the 1950s, as economic growth began to take hold, Luis Muñoz Marín and others began to feel concerned that something was being lost. As a result of this concern, Puerto Ricans decided to preserve the traditions and the cultural heritage of their people. One part of this effort was the creation of the Institute of Puerto Rican Culture. Programs at the institute were set up to encourage artists in all forms.

The two strongest threads in Puerto Rico's artistic life are music and literature. In both arts, the life of the individual and the struggles of the island and its people show themselves as two sides of the same coin.

There are some fascinating forms of folk music on the island. In the mountains, there is a form called the *décima*. Singers get together and compete with each other in making up rhymes about particular people or events important to people. They have to create their verses on the spot.

Puerto Ricans of African heritage who live along the coast have a similar form called the *plena*. Plenas

Puerto Rico's folk culture still thrives in Jayuya in central Puerto Rico.

Pablo Casals established Puerto Rico's annual Casals Festival of classical music.

also deal with current events out of the lives of the people. The event could be a natural disaster like a fire or a flood. It could be some sporting event. Plenas have a strong beat and are accompanied by hand-held rhythm instruments.

Today, the most popular form of music that began in Puerto Rico is *salsa*, which means "spicy sauce." It is as loud and as lively as rock 'n' roll. Salsa is Spanish and African with a touch of American "Big Band" jazz.

Puerto Rico has produced formal music, too. Its greatest composer was probably Juan Morel Campos, who lived in the second half of the nineteenth century. His most popular works were *danzas*, or dances.

In 1956 Puerto Rico's musical life got a boost from Pablo Casals. Casals was a world-famous cellist, composer, and conductor. He was born in Spain, but his mother was Puerto Rican. From 1956 until he died in 1973, Casals made his home on the island. He started the Casals Festival. This festival, held yearly in June, brings world-class musicians to the city of San Juan.

Casals also worked to create a first-class symphony orchestra for Puerto Rico. At first, musicians had to be brought in from outside. Later, Casals founded the Conservatory of Music to train classical musicians in Puerto Rico.

Literature in Puerto Rico often has been directly connected with political and social struggles. It's not unusual to find artists in public life. One of Puerto Rico's greatest political leaders, Luis Muñoz Marín, was also a poet. But the tradition began long before him.

In the middle of the nineteenth century, Manuel A. Alonso wrote stories and poetry that recorded the life of the jíbaro. Alejandro Tapia y Rivera wrote excellent works in many forms, including a play called *The Quadroon Woman*, which dealt with racial prejudice.

Eugenio María de Hostos was a very important voice in Puerto Rico. He was a philosopher, a student of law, a teacher, and a writer. He wrote children's stories, scholarly articles, and everything in between. Hostos believed strongly that there should be an independent federation of Caribbean states.

Luis Palés Matos lived from 1898 until 1959. In the later part of his life, he was inspired by the lives of African Puerto Ricans. His lyrical poetry shows that influence.

An important group of writers was called the Generation of the Thirties. They were interested in exploring what it meant to be Puerto Rican. Among the group were writers such as Antonia Pedreira, Tomás Blanco, and Enrique Laguerre.

After World War II, much of Puerto Rican writing dealt with the experience of immigrants. Playwright René Marques's best-known work, *La Carreta*, tells of a family's immigration to New York City and the trouble they face when they move back to Puerto Rico. The

Dancers at the LeLoLai festival in San Juan celebrate traditional culture and music.

The Tapia Theatre in Old San Juan was built in 1832. It is named for playwright Alejandro Tapia y Rivera.

lives of Puerto Ricans in New York and Chicago became a part of the total cultural heritage of Puerto Rico.

The art of Puerto Rico was born out of Spain and Africa. American influences have also been added to this unique mix. The island's art has been fed by the joys of life in the sun and by the pain of a people's search for freedom. It may offer celebration but seldom escape. In Puerto Rico, art is not a luxury. It is a tool to be used as well as enjoyed.

Half of Earth's species of plants and animals live in rain forests. These falls are in Puerto Rico's El Yunque rain forest.

Hope in Playa de Ponce

Although the economy of Puerto Rico has developed rapidly, unemployment has always been high. There are still pockets of poverty where young people can't find jobs. This may cause them to lose faith in themselves. Sor Isolina, a Catholic nun and sister of a former governor, described the problem. "When you don't have anything to look forward to, when you don't have any opportunities, then you become discouraged. You become self-defeated."

Sor Isolina had witnessed the discouragement of those with no hope. She saw it very near her own home, in the waterfront neighborhood called Playa de Ponce. It was there that she founded a community center. The idea behind the center is to help people find respect and dignity. She encourages them to know their own worth. In this way they can learn to help themselves.

When the center first opened, there were problems. It took time and understanding for Sor Isolina to gain the confidence of the young people. "In fact," she said, "they came twice to our offices and they stole from us. But the mothers came that day and they were so embarrassed. They said, 'Put them in jail, take them away!' Then I said, 'No, that is not the way. You have to stand by your children right now.' "

One of the young troublemakers was a boy named Torpedo. It took some work to make him realize how much he needed what the center had to offer. "I was in a lot of trouble," he explained. "The sister talked to me about my problems and said I shouldn't bring them into this community. So I decided to straighten out. But I owe it to her. She counseled me and showed me right from wrong."

Torpedo began to study photography at the center. He had a good teacher, and he learned quickly. The work he was able to produce gave him a sense of his own worth, something that Sor Isolina was hoping for.

Then, through his photography, Torpedo spread the word. He took pictures of his friends, and they grew to respect his gift for photography. Torpedo told how this happened.

"They see me with the camera and ask me to take pictures of them laughing and talking. Then I tell them that I want them to pose. I want portraits—real portraits—and I don't want them fooling and joking around. I think they understand now, because when the pictures are developed, they are really anxious to see them."

Sor Isolina's community center is a good example of the way hope can bring people new life. Sometimes hope

These schoolchildren walk across a plaza with their teacher in tow.

An entire culture can be portrayed in an artful photograph such as this one.

is all it takes to make people believe in themselves and their futures. Sor Isolina described how the camera can show people a brand-new way of seeing things. "To us, photography is a way of learning—to learn the reality of their life around them, to make them also beautiful. It was in the Metropolitan Museum of New York that we had this exhibit. And people came around and looked at the houses and said, 'Oh, what ugly houses!' And this little girl came over and said to this lady, 'Oh, no, that is not ugly. That is my house. And that's a beautiful picture, if you look at it.' "

When people learn to see the beauty in their own lives, a sense of worth and faith in themselves follows.

This church is the Cathedral of Our Lady of Guadalupe in Playa de Ponce. In 1754 the Pope of the Roman Catholic Church declared the Virgin of Guadalupe to be the patron and protector of Spanish America.

The Promise of Puerto Rico

In Puerto Rico, two streams, one economic and one cultural, flow toward the future. Within the last few decades, the people of Puerto Rico have taken major steps toward improving their economy and preserving their way of life. Beginning in the 1940s, Puerto Ricans found the courage to dramatically improve the quality of life on the island. In doing so, they showed creativity, intelligence, and farsightedness.

Operation Bootstrap was a movement toward economic well-being. Faced with poor living conditions, the commonwealth decided to move forward. It took hold of itself with both hands and pulled itself into the modern industrial world. Puerto Rico developed a skilled workforce and attracted business and industries. In doing so, Puerto Rico vastly improved the lives of its people.

Then, in the midst of this progress, Puerto Ricans did something few states or nations have had the wisdom to do. They realized they might be losing their unique cultural heritage. So they established programs

Independence party supporters wave Puerto Rican flags during a rally just before the referendum vote in November 1993.

The plants this man is unloading may grace some of the interior patios that are so characteristic of Spanish American architecture.

and organizations that preserve the culture and enrich their lives.

The wisdom that led Puerto Rico to transform its economy and protect its heritage will surely be tested in the future. Its workers earn an hourly wage much lower than that of the mainland. Its unemployment rate is higher than that of the United States. Many islanders oppose the North American Free Trade Agreement (NAFTA). They fear it will cause firms to move their operations—and jobs—to Mexico, where wages are lower.

But Puerto Rico's people can meet the challenges. The promise of Puerto Rico lies in its willingness to take a good hard look at itself, to weigh alternatives, and to foresee consequences. These abilities are the key to its future.

Important Historical Events

1493   Christopher Columbus claims Puerto Rico for Spain. He names the island San Juan Bautista.

1508   Spanish explorer Juan Ponce de León leads a group of Spanish settlers to the island.

1509   Ponce de León becomes the governor of the settlement.

1515   Sugar cane is first planted.

1595   Sir Francis Drake leads an unsuccessful attack on the forts El Morro Castle and San Cristóbal.

1598   The English attack and capture San Juan. They hold it for five months.

1625   The Dutch capture and burn San Juan.

1797   The British fail in their attempt to take control of San Juan.

1868   Puerto Ricans rebel against Spanish rule.

1897   Puerto Ricans win a certain measure of home rule when Spain makes Puerto Rico a Spanish dominion.

1898   The Spanish-American War breaks out. American forces bombard San Juan and land at Guanica on July 25. Spain gives up Puerto Rico to the United States on December 10, under the terms of the Treaty of Paris.

1900   Congress creates a civil government for Puerto Rico.

1917   Congress passes the Jones Act, which makes Puerto Ricans citizens of the United States.

1940   Operation Bootstrap begins.

1946   Jesús T. Piñero is appointed by President Harry S. Truman as the first island-born governor of Puerto Rico.

1947   Congress expands the Jones Act to allow Puerto Ricans to elect their own governor.

1949   Luis Muñoz Marín becomes the first elected governor in Puerto Rico.

1950   Congress passes a law allowing Puerto Rico to write its own constitution.

1952   Puerto Rico adopts its constitution and becomes a self-governing commonwealth of the United States.

1960   Puerto Rico undergoes tremendous industrial growth with the help of the Economic Development Administration, or *Fomento*, begun in the 1950s.

1967   More than sixty percent of Puerto Rican voters favor retaining commonwealth status rather than becoming a state or an independent country.

1968   Luis A. Ferré is elected governor of Puerto Rico on the platform of statehood for the island.

1972   Rafael Hernández Colón defeats Luis Ferré in his bid for reelection.

1976   Carlos Romero Barceló, San Juan mayor and New Progressive party candidate, is elected governor.

1980   Carlos Romero Barceló is reelected.

1989   Hurricane Hugo strikes Puerto Rico, killing 12 people and causing $1 billion in damage.

1993   In the first political status referendum since 1967, 48 percent of Puerto Ricans vote to remain a commonwealth and 46 percent support statehood.

1994   An oil barge strikes a coral reef off San Juan, spilling 750,000 gallons of diesel fuel.

The flag was designed in the late eighteenth century by Puerto Ricans living in New York. It was first raised in 1952, the year Puerto Rico became a commonwealth of the United States. The red, white, and blue colors reflect those of the United States flag.

Puerto Rico Almanac

Official Name. Commonwealth of Puerto Rico

Capital. San Juan

Bird. Reinita

Flower. Maga

Tree. Ceiba

Motto. *Joannes Est Nomen Ejus* (John Is His Name)

Song. "La Borinqueña"

Abbreviations. P.R. (traditional); PR (postal)

Commonwealth Status. July 25, 1952

Government. Congress: Resident Commissioner (votes only in committees). Commonwealth Legislature: senators, 27; representatives, 53. Municipalities: 78

Area. 3,515 sq mi (9,103 sq km)

Greatest Distances. north/south, 39 mi (63 km); east/west, 111 mi (179 km). Coastline: 311 mi (501 km)

Elevation. Highest: Cerro de Punta, 4,389 ft (1,338 m). Lowest: sea level, along the coast

Population. 1990 Census: 3,522,037 (10% increase over 1980). Density: 1,004 persons per sq mi (387 persons per sq km). Distribution: 67% urban, 33% rural. 1980 Census: 3,196,520

Economy. *Agriculture:* sugar cane, milk, poultry, eggs, beef cattle, bananas, plantains, pineapple, coffee. *Fishing:* lobster. *Manufacturing:* medicines, electrical machinery and equipment, processed foods, scientific instruments, nonelectrical machinery, clothing. *Mining:* stone, gravel, lime

Bird: Reinita

Flower: Maga

Annual Events

★ Carnival in Ponce (February)

★ Emancipation Day (March)

★ Albonito Flower Festival (June)

★ Casals Festival in San Juan (June)

★ Commonwealth Day (July)

★ Columbus Day (October)

★ Discovery Day (November)

★ Hatillo Festival of the Masks (December)

★ Patron Saint Festivals (year-round)

Places to Visit

★ Arecibo Observatory in northwest Puerto Rico

★ Caribbean National Forest (El Yunque)

★ El Morro Fortress, near San Juan

★ La Fortalenza in Old San Juan

★ Luquillo Beach in northeast Puerto Rico

★ Phosphorescent Bay at La Parguera

★ Porta Coeli Chapel and Museum of Religious Art in San Germán

★ Ponce Museum of Art in Ponce

★ San Juan Cathedral in San Juan